Published by Macdonald Children's Books
Simon & Schuster International Group
Wolsey House, Wolsey Road
Hemel Hempstead HP2 4SS

First published in Great Britain by
Macdonald Children's Books 1989

Originally published as 'je regard, je comprends . . . L'air'
by Editions des Deux Coqs d'Or, Paris

© 1988 Editions des Deux Coqs d'Or

British Library Cataloguing in Publication Data

Averous, Pierre
   Air.
   1. Air. Juvenile literature
   I. Title II. De Seabra, Catherine III. Series IV. Je regarde,
   je comprends l'air. *English*
   551.5'1

ISBN 0 356 16857 3 (HB)
ISBN 0 356 16896 4 (PB)

Printed in Great Britain by
The Eagle Press, Blantyre

In the Picture
Air

Pierre Avérous   Catherine de Seabra

Macdonald Children's Books

Contents

Pore over the large pictures . . . and then turn the page to discover something new. Look carefully and you'll find out more about the world we live in.

Turn the page and find out about the wind . . .

Moving in the wind

Like a giant draught

If you leave the windows wide open at home you will make a draught. Sheets of paper fly away and doors slam. There are giant draughts in the sky too. Of course, they don't blow through a window. They often come from the sea. They blow across the land, slip between mountains, and rush along the streets. You feel these giant draughts as the wind on your face. Often they have come from far away.

When the wind blows

When the air is still, there is no wind. We don't notice it, because air is invisible and has no smell. We forget about it. But we can feel the air when it starts moving across the countryside, blowing leaves and kites high in the sky. Often you will see clouds moving in the sky above. It is the wind that pushes them along. The wind which blows in the sky and the wind which blows along the ground do not always come from the same place.

It wears away rocks

The gusts of wind that you feel on your face also move along the ground. When the wind is very strong, it lifts up grains of soil and sand and hurls them against rocks. As the grains rub along the rocks, they slowly wear the rocks away. Gradually, the rocks become smoother and are worn into strange shapes. In the deserts, there are magnificent rocks which have been shaped in this way by the work of the wind.

A wind-sock in the wind

What a strange flag! It looks like a shirt-sleeve or a trouser leg. But it's not there just for fun. It is called a wind-sock and it shows the direction of the wind, in the same way that a weathervane does. Wind-socks are brightly coloured and can be seen from far away. The bigger and fuller the wind-sock is, the stronger the wind.

Sailing in the wind

It can be very windy on the open sea. There is nothing to stop the wind. There are no trees or mountains to slow it down or to change its direction. Sailors have learnt how to use the wind by putting up large sails. They fill with wind, and as the wind blows, it pushes the boat forwards. Some sailing boats have several masts and huge sails. They can sail across oceans and go round the world.

A swirling wind

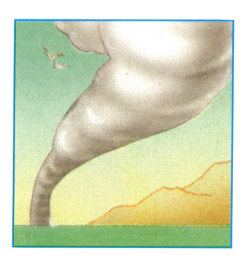

At sea, there are areas where the wind blows so strongly that it spins round like a spinning top! It is like a small whirlwind which corkscrews down from the clouds and whips up the waves with an incredible force. It is called a water spout. Much bigger whirlwinds are called hurricanes. They are huge and violent and can sweep across whole countries. Hurricanes are formed over tropical seas when the air is very hot.

And now, let's go into the sky in an aeroplane . . .

Flying in the air

A giant kite

Have you ever watched a kite flying in the sky and thought you'd like to be able to fly like that? A hang-glider is rather like a kite. It floats and glides above the countryside. The person is attached firmly under the glider. But don't ever try to do this on your own, it is very dangerous. You need to be taught how to use a hang-glider before attempting to hang-glide by yourself.

Carried on a draught

If you were a sheet of paper, you wouldn't have any problem flying. All you need is a small draught and you're up and away. You start your journey and you float, turn round, and fly off again. But you are not made of paper! And flying is not so easy. People have always wanted to fly, but it has taken us thousands of years to be able to build a machine which could take us into the air.

We need wings to fly

Butterflies and birds know how to fly. They flap their wings, and take off. They can twist and turn as they want, flying quickly and skilfully. They have special muscles to help them fly which are very strong for their size. Our arms would not be strong enough for us to fly, even if we fixed wings to them.

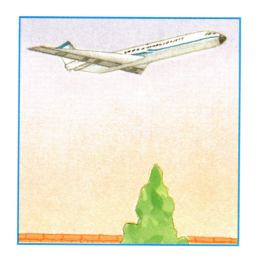

Planes can fly too

But planes don't have muscles! They don't flap their wings to fly. Instead, they have powerful engines which push or thrust them forward. Their large, strong wings help the plane to stay in the air. The pilot lifts or lowers small flaps fixed to the edge of the wings and tail to make the plane climb or dive, and to turn.

The nose of a plane

To fly fast, you have to push the air aside. Birds do this by pushing forward with their heads and beaks. Fish do the same, pushing through the water to swim fast. In the same way, the sharper the nose of the plane, the more quickly it pushes away the air and the faster the plane moves through the air. Very fast planes have very sharp noses.

Slowed down by the air

Some flowers have very unusual seeds. For example when lime and maple seeds are ripe, they fall to the ground. But they fall in an interesting way. They are attached to a large wing, so they glide through the air and drop slowly to the ground. A parachute works in the same way. It stops the parachutist falling to the ground too quickly.

Now come down to the river for a breath of fresh air . . .

Take a deep breath

A strange mixture

You can't hold air in your hands. It isn't solid. You can't drink it out of a glass either. It isn't liquid. It is a gas. In fact it is a mixture of several gases which are all invisible and which don't have a smell. The most useful gas in the air is oxygen. That's the one we need to breathe. The most plentiful gas is called nitrogen. The air also contains a little carbon dioxide. This is a gas we don't need and so we breathe it out again.

We breathe the air

It's lovely to sit by the river! The sound of the river soothes you and sends you to sleep. When you are asleep, your chest is always moving a little. It goes up and down: you are breathing. Inside, your lungs are taking air in and pushing it out, without stopping day or night. Your body needs air as much as it needs food. Without air, you would not live.

All animals breathe

Cows, birds and lizards all breathe like us. Their lungs sort out what is in the air. They keep the oxygen. This travels in the blood through the whole body. The lungs breathe out the unwanted air. Beetles, snails and worms breathe too, like all the animals which live on land. But they do not have real lungs. Instead the air enters their body through their skin.

Let's open the windows!

At home, everyone is breathing in and out all day long. The air slowly becomes stuffy and stale. It contains less and less oxygen and more and more carbon dioxide. If we did not do anything about it, we would start feeling ill. That's why it is important to open the windows often to let the fresh air in.

Plants need air too

Flowers and trees look so pretty in spring, as the green leaves start to appear! But did you know that plants breathe, just like you? Although they don't have lungs, they take in oxygen through their leaves and stems. Green plants also need carbon dioxide to grow. It is like a food for them. But no animal could live on it!

Fish don't like air

When you have caught a fish, you can see it wriggling in the basket. But the fish will eventually die, because it does not breathe like us. Fish don't have lungs to breathe in oxygen. Instead they have gills which are adapted to take in the oxygen from the water. This is the only way they can breathe.

Come and find out more about the weather . . .

19

Moving air makes the weathe

Playing leap-frog

Above the Earth there are huge masses of air. Some are warm and some are cold. They are always moving and playing leap-frog around the Earth. As the air moves from warm masses to cool masses, it forms winds. Balloons and birds use the movements of the air above the seas and mountains to glide in the sky.

Air is full of water

Although you may not be able to feel it, the air always has some moisture in it. Usually the droplets are so tiny that you cannot see them. This is when you see a bright blue sky. In some parts of the sky where it is colder, the droplets in the air bump into each other and stick together. Eventually they will form a cloud, .which may bring us rain.

Making a rainbow

What a beautiful rainbow! But however hard you try, you will never be able to catch it. A rainbow is formed by the Sun's rays in the sky. Nobody can touch them. When it rains and the Sun is shining at the same time, the rays of sunlight pass through each drop of rain. They separate out into the colours of the rainbow: violet, indigo, blue, green, yellow, orange, and red. But as soon as the rain stops, all the colours disappear.

Air colours the sky

Look at the sky when the Sun sets. The wonderful pink or orange colours are made by the air and the Sun's rays. Before the rays reach you, they go through a thick layer of air. During this journey, the blue colour in the rays disappears: the blue fills up the sky in the countries where it is still light. But the orange in the rays carries on its journey towards you. It sets the sky on fire.

Lightning in the sky

This balloon has a fork of lightning and a big black storm cloud on it. When there is a real storm, the wind blows and the rain pours down! In the middle of the clouds, the air is so shaken up that sometimes it makes a huge spark of electricity. We see a flash of lightning in the sky. The lightning heats the air around so much that the air makes a deafening noise: that's when you hear thunder.

Forecasting the weather

What a wonderful journey in the balloon! But the thermometer shows the temperature is dropping a little. And as soon as the wind gets up, the tiny windmill fixed to the basket starts turning fast. There are instruments like these all over the world. They help us to tell what the weather will be like. These are the tools of the scientists who study the weather. They are called meteorologists

Come for a change of air in the mountains . . .

A layer of air called the

Air surrounds the Earth

In Australia, America or in the middle of the largest ocean, there is always air. The air surrounds the Earth. During the day, it protects the Earth from the powerful rays of the Sun. During the night, the air stops the Earth getting too cold, in the same way that this tea-cosy keeps the teapot warm on the table. This layer of air around the Earth is called the atmosphere.

In the mountains

If you go for a walk in the mountains, you will discover the most wonderful scenery: pine forests, snow-fields, animals you may never have seen before. People who climb right to the top of the highest peaks in the world get tired very quickly. It is because they can't get enough air. The higher you climb, the less air there is. And in the part of the sky where planes fly, there is hardly any air at all.

Air is not heavy

This is a barometer. We look at it to see what the weather will be like. The barometer can tell us this by measuring the weight of the air above it, because the atmosphere which surrounds the Earth weighs down on everything. The air even weighs down on your shoulders. You don't notice it because you are used to it. Air is not heavy. The amount of air in an empty bottle is lighter than a pea.

atmosphere

It is full of dust

The air is full of the dust from the countryside. Sometimes it gets in your eyes. Some dust particles are quite big, like the fine powder called pollen, which you find in flowers. The air can carry the pollen over a long distance. The air can also carry seeds hanging from their tiny parachutes. Where the seeds settle, new plants will grow.

It can be dirty

The air carries away smoke from fires, car exhausts and factory chimneys. It even carries away the thick grey dust and ash that explodes into the air when a volcano erupts. In places where there is too much smoke, the air eventually gets dirty. Such an atmosphere can make the plants, animals and people living there ill. It is important to keep the air of the Earth as clean as possible.

Shooting stars in the sky

Here's an unusual shirt with shooting stars on it. Have you ever seen some at night? They look like small specks of light which shoot across a sky full of stars. In fact shooting stars are made of small pieces of rock which come from Space. As they travel towards the Earth, the atmosphere rubs against them. It rubs so hard that it sets them on fire. We can see their glowing tails in the sky.

Happy birthday! Come and open your presents . . .

Strange air

Warm air rises

Today it is cold. The radiator has been turned on so that it will be warm at the party. The radiator is hot and warms the air next to it. When the air is warm, it rises up to the ceiling. If you put your hand above the radiator, you can feel it through your fingers. Look at the ribbons too: they are floating in the warm air, like little flags.

Air makes the fire burn

Everybody is here. Now we can light the candles on the cake. You may not realize it, but you need some air to light the candles. Fire needs oxygen from the air in order to burn. Without oxygen, the candles, the gas cooker or the gas fire couldn't burn. In fact, nothing could.

It makes engines work

The engine of the boat is very noisy, like the engine of a car. The noise comes from inside the engine where the petrol mixes up with some air. A spark sets the mixture on fire and bang! The mixture explodes. These explosions happen very quickly and start the engine turning. That's what makes the noise you can hear.

We can see through it

A pair of binoculars, what a fabulous present! If you hold them steady in front of your eyes, you can see far away: birds in their nests, planes high in the sky or footballers on the other side of the pitch. This is because we can see through the air which surrounds the Earth. We say it is transparent. The air turns pale blue when you look far away, for instance if you look towards the horizon or high into the sky.

Air can be squeezed

Look at these divers with their masks and bottles of oxygen on their back. They have to carry the air they need with them so that they can breathe under water. The air is squeezed, or compressed, into bottles. Even so they need a lot of air. When divers need to use the air, they put a pipe from the bottle into their mouths and open a special tap. This lets out the amount of air the divers need.

We can get rid of air

Let's open the packet of peanuts. It's quite flat. As soon as you make a hole with a pair of scissors, you will hear a noise as the air rushes into the packet. Before the packet was sealed, a machine sucked out all the air from it. We call this a vacuum. This helps to keep the peanuts longer. If they were left in the air, they would go bad. Sometimes it is very handy to know how to get rid of air.

Look for air in the play room . . .

Air is very useful

A balloon full of air

Look! Take this balloon and blow it up as much as you can. It gets bigger and bigger. The balloon is like a bag full of air. When you blow into it, you fill it up with the air that you have breathed in. But don't blow it up too much because it might burst!

On a cushion of air

Car tyres are full of air just like balloons. The tyre is like a cushion around each wheel. Because of the tyre we do not feel the bumps in the road so much. A hovercraft uses a cushion of air too. A hovercraft is a cross between a car and a plane but it doesn't have any wheels. It moves by sliding along on a giant cushion of air which is pumped up by powerful fans.

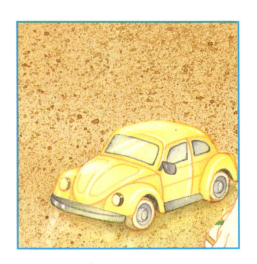

A drill uses air

This workman is using a pneumatic drill which is a very useful tool for breaking up concrete, for example. A pneumatic drill needs air to work. A pipe fills the drill with air. Inside the drill, the air is pressed down hard or compressed and then quickly released. When the air comes out, it pushes down on the drill in the same way that you bang in a nail with a hammer. The drill breaks up the ground. This movement is repeated over and over again.

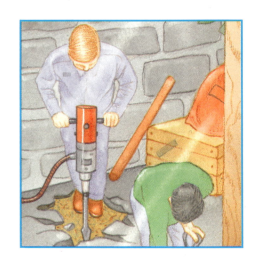

A fan makes a breeze

It is so hot today, it would be nice to feel a breeze. To make a breeze without too much effort, you only have to open up a fan and to move it gently to and fro. A slight movement of the hand and a gentle breeze cools your face. In hot countries, people often use fans.

Drying things quickly

The painting is finished. You can use a hair dryer to dry it fast. The hot air quickly dries the paint, like the wind dries the washing. The warmer the air, the quicker the water dries up. But be careful not to damage your painting!

Engineers use air

The strange clouds around this car are made out of coloured air! Engineers who build new cars or planes use a wind tunnel to help them get the best design for the body. They design the body and test it in the wind tunnel. If the air which slides over the car doesn't make any coloured swirls, then the engineers know they have found the right shape. It is amazing how useful the air can be!

Now let's use the air to make some music . . .

Air brings us sounds

It whistles

Blow in the recorder and play a tune. If you cover all the holes with your fingers, you get a low sound. But if you leave a few holes open, the sound is higher. The air goes through the mouthpiece of the recorder and down the pipe until it can escape. It comes out through the holes which are not covered. The note you play changes depending on the length of the air's journey through the pipe.

We need it to speak

Do you like talking, shouting and singing? Again you need air to do this! At the bottom of your throat, there are two stiff pieces of skin or membranes, called the vocal cords. Without you noticing it, they are opening and closing all the time. The air you blow out when you speak makes these cords vibrate. The sounds echo up your throat and then come out of your mouth. Your lips then move to talk, shout or sing.

It vibrates

The drum also makes its sound because of air. When the drumstick hits the drum, it makes the skin stretched over the drum vibrate, in the same way the windows vibrate when a big lorry goes by in the street. The skin moves backwards and forwards very quickly – so fast you can't see it. When you hit the drum, the air inside the drum is given a 'knock'. You hear the bang of the drum.

It carries sounds

Outside, the street is full of the noise of cars. If you don't want to hear it, shut the window. Then the people in the street won't be able to hear the music that you are playing. The music, your voices, the noise of car engines, all these travel through the air. The air carries the noise. Window-panes and walls stop the sounds from travelling. They protect us from the noise.

It helps us to hear

The air is like a wonderful magician: it helps us make musical sounds, shout and speak. It also makes explosions or thunder! And that's not all: it then carries all these sounds into your ears! There it makes a small membrane vibrate. This membrane is called the ear-drum because it is like the skin of a drum. When the ear-drum vibrates, it sends a signal to the brain. The brain then tells us what we are hearing. Without ear-drums you couldn't hear.

Sounds we cannot hear

The bats are awake. Normally, they like dark places and only fly at night. But they cannot see in the dark. To make sure they don't bump into anything, they make high squeaking sounds. We cannot hear them because our ears are not adapted to these sounds. When the sounds hit something, for example a wall, they bounce back as an echo. The bat hears the echo and knows to avoid the wall. Dogs also can hear sounds that we cannot hear.

And what if there was no air . . . ?

When there is no air

People wear spacesuits

Far away from the Earth, there is no air. There is nothing. When astronauts travel in Space and want to get out of their shuttle or capsule, they have to wear special spacesuits. These spacesuits have air inside for the astronauts to breathe. If they didn't wear spacesuits they would not be able to survive.

Flags don't fly

When there isn't the slightest bit of wind, flags cannot fly. If you want to put a flag in Space, you have to make it taut or stiff. You can do this by holding it in position with small sticks. You can also make the flag out of a thin sheet of metal.

There is no noise

You know now that it's the air which makes sounds and which carries them to our ears. In Space, sounds cannot exist. Even the astronauts' tools and the engines of their machines work in total silence. People sometimes find it surprising not to be able to hear anything.

The sky is all dark

On the Earth, during the daytime, the Sun's rays light up the blue sky and the clouds, and everything is colourful. For the astronauts, the sky is always dark, even during the day, because there is no air or clouds! And you cannot see any colour.

Burning and freezing

When there is no air, nothing can stop the Sun's rays. They are so strong that they make things very hot. On the other hand, in the shade, things get so cold that they freeze. Satellites which travel in Space have to be very strong to be able to cope with the intense heat and cold. And the astronauts' spacesuits have to be well heated!

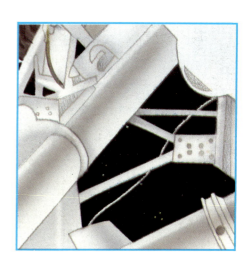

Protected from the Sun

Without air, the Sun is very dangerous. It not only burns, but its light also dazzles. Astronauts have to wear a special eyeshade fitted on their helmet to protect their eyes. This protects their eyes better than the best sunglasses. You can see that it is not easy to walk around in Space. It is a good thing that there is air around the Earth!

Some questions and answers

How does the warm air rise in the sky?

When a mass of air gets warmer, it becomes bigger. We say it expands. We cannot see it because the air is invisible. As warm air expands, it rises above the cold air which surrounds it, like a very light air-bubble rises up to the surface of the water. There is one mass of warm air that you can see: it's a hot air balloon. This beautiful flying machine can carry people in the sky. To make it fly, you need to fill up a giant bag with air warmed by a flame. When the bag is full of warm air, it makes the balloon lighter. It can take off and fly away with its passengers.

How does the air warm up?

All around the Earth, there are some places which are warmer than others. The ground is always warmed by the Sun. The air above these places warms up like the air above a radiator. Then the air rises in the sky. Beneath it, colder air comes in to take its place. Sometimes, according to the place or the time of the year, the sea is warmer than the land and the waves warm up the air above. There are always places which are warmer than others. It is here that the air's journey begins.

Why is it important not to dirty the air?

We must be very careful to keep the air clean, and not to dirty or pollute it with the smoke from factories and cars. Polluted air could make us ill. But it could also make people ill who live far away from us. The air which is above us at the moment will be blown away, in a week or a month, to somewhere else. Other people will breathe in our polluted air! At the moment you may be breathing in the very clean air which has taken all its oxygen from above the forests in Africa or South America.

about the air

Why doesn't the weight of the air crush us?

Put your hand flat on the ground. One kilo of air is pressing on each of your nails. Your body is used to it. Inside your body, your blood is pressing back just as much, but in the other direction. And so you don't feel anything at all.

Is it true that air can be liquid?

Yes, it is true, but you will not find it in nature. Only scientists know how to make liquid air, using special equipment. They take some normal air and press it down very hard or compress it. At the same time, they cool down the compressed air very quickly. In this way, they turn the gases in the air into a liquid: it flows like water. You can pour it in a glass or fill a bottle. Liquid air is much colder than ice. It is so cold that it would hurt you if you were to touch it.

Is there air on the other planets in the Solar System?

No, there is not. The air that you breathe in, the atmosphere, only exists on the Earth. Other planets are too small to keep gases close to them. They do not have any atmosphere. Mercury for instance, the planet which is closest to the Sun, has no atmosphere. The Moon which turns around the Earth has no atmosphere either. Venus, however, is the same size as our planet and it is surrounded by a strange atmosphere which is so thick that we cannot see the surface of the planet through it, even with the most powerful of telescopes. But we couldn't breathe in Venus's atmosphere: it is very hot, very heavy and does not contain any oxygen, only deadly gases which would kill us! The atmosphere on Mars, Jupiter or Saturn would not be suitable either. Air as we know it only exists on the Earth.